HIP-HOP Biographies

KANYE WEST

SADDLEBACK PUBLISHING

HIP-HOP Biographies

Chris Brown
Drake
50 Cent
Jay-Z
Nicki Minaj

Pitbull
Rihanna
Usher
Lil Wayne
Kanye West

SADDLEBACK
PUBLISHING
www.sdlback.com

ISBN-13: 978-1-62250-016-1
ISBN-10: 1-62250-016-4
eBook: 978-1-61247-697-1

Printed in Guangzhou, China
NOR/1112/CA21201417
17 16 15 14 13   1 2 3 4 5

Table of Contents

Timeline

1998: Kanye sells his first beat to Jermaine Dupri.

1977: Kanye West is born in Atlanta, Georgia.

1999: Kanye is the *producer* for Foxy Brown, Lil Kim, and more.

1987: Kanye moves to China.

1991: Kanye gets his first keyboard, turntable, and mixer.

2000: Kanye produces a track for Jay-Z.

2002: Kanye crashes his car and nearly dies.

Roc-a-Fella signs Kanye to a recording contract.

1996: Kanye drops out of college to focus on music.

Sony Music interviews Kanye but does not offer him a *contract*.

2004: Kanye's *debut* album, *The College Dropout*, is released.

2005: Kanye releases his second album, *Late Registration*.

2006: Kanye wins three Grammy Awards.

2007: Kanye competes with 50 Cent to see who sells the most albums.

Kanye releases *Graduation*.

Kanye's mother dies.

2011: Kanye releases *Watch the Throne* with Jay-Z.

Kanye holds his first Paris fashion show.

2012: Kim Kardashian and Kanye start dating.

Kanye the Icon

In the *tabloids*, Kanye West is known as an overconfident musician and fashion designer. In the music business, he is considered by many as a genius.

Kanye calls himself the voice of a generation.

He is a very successful producer and rap artist. Kanye, or Yeezy, even calls himself the voice of a generation.
He said, "Someone could be a better rapper, dance better. But culturally impacting? When you look back, ... who's the icon at the end of the day?"

Kanye is arrogant. But he is so successful that he has a right to brag. He is known as a perfectionist in terms of music. He works on his sounds until they are exactly how he thinks they should sound. The perfectionism has paid off. By 2012 he had won eighteen Grammy Awards. In the United States, he has sold over thirty million songs just over digital sellers like iTunes. (This does not count actual CDs sold in stores!) He is one of the best-selling and most-awarded musical artists of all time. And he reached this level of success before he even turned forty years old.

It may be the way Kanye experiences music that makes him so special. He has a condition called synesthesia. People with synesthesia get more information when they see, feel, hear, taste, or smell something than others do. In Kanye's case, he sees the sounds he hears. In an interview, Kanye described what this is like for him. He said, "When I was in grammar school, I had a colored-pencil drawing of my take on synesthesia. I knew I could see sounds and shapes. I can see sound in front of me." So Kanye writes and makes music that looks as good to him as it sounds.

Donda Williams was raised in Oklahoma. She was the youngest of four children. Her parents both worked long hours to provide for their family. The Williams family lived in the southern United States in the 1950s and 60s. This meant that they had to face *segregation*. Restrooms, drinking fountains, and seats on buses were marked as "White Only" and "Negro Only." It was against the law for African Americans to defy segregation laws. But Donda's mother ignored the signs. She was very confident, and people who would complain or have her arrested left her alone instead. Donda grew up with the same kind of confidence.

Donda's parents understood that an education would give their children opportunities that they did not have. She attended college and earned a doctorate degree. She taught business classes and went to graduate school.

Ray West grew up all over the United States and in Spain. His father was in the military, so he was stationed at different military bases. Ray also grew up with segregation. When his family had to move to a new base, they often slept in their car. The West family could not find hotels that allowed African Americans to rent a room. Because many restaurants would not serve them, they would eat sandwiches in the car.

Ray went to college and became active in African American causes. He became a member of the Black Panther Party. The organization worked to gain equality for African Americans in all parts of their lives. The group was considered very radical, but it also helped African Americans gain rights that they did not have before.

Donda Williams was Kanye's mother.

Donda and Ray met when they were both working for Spelman College in Atlanta, Georgia. They dated for just three months before they married. For four years they lived happily, remodeling homes around Atlanta and working on their careers. In 1976 Donda became pregnant. Ray was not sure he wanted to be a father.

Donda and Kanye moved to this neighborhood in Chicago.

Kanye Omari West was born on June 8, 1977, in Atlanta. In the months after Kanye's birth, Ray spent more time at work and less time at home. Donda did not want to stay married to someone whose work was more important than his family. Donda and Ray separated before Kanye was a year old. When Kanye was three years old, Donda and Ray divorced.

Donda moved to Chicago to take a job as an English professor. When it was time for Kanye to start kindergarten, she found the Vanderpoel Magnet School. They had teachers who helped develop students' talents in art and music. Kanye was talented in both art and music, so Donda paid for private lessons in both. Kanye saw his father in the summers when school was out.

In 1987 Donda was given an amazing opportunity. Her college would exchange professors with a university in China. Donda moved to Nanjing, China. Kanye went with her and attended a local school. He was the only foreign student in class. Because he did not speak Chinese, they placed him in first grade. But he quickly learned the language and moved up to his normal grade. The children in his school would pay Kanye to break dance for them, so he always had spare change for treats in the neighborhood markets.

11

Young Producer

When Donda and Kanye moved back to Chicago, their neighborhood was not safe. Kanye's bike tires were slashed because he would not give the bike to neighborhood thieves. Kids were being attacked for the jackets and shoes that they wore. Donda moved to a safer neighborhood.

Kanye became passionate about hip-hop music. Neither Donda nor Ray were very excited about his interest in this style of music. Donda did not like the bad behavior that rap songs often talked about. When Kanye went to hip-hop concerts, she would follow him to be sure he stayed out of trouble. Ray hated the profanity in many rap songs. The songs often used words that were insulting to African Americans as well as women. Ray told his son, "You know that's not where you came from. You know that's not how you were raised."

Even with his parents' concern, Kanye loved rap. When he was twelve, he wrote a rap about Dr. Seuss's *Green Eggs and Ham*. Kanye was desperate to record the song. They checked at recording studios around the Chicago area. The going rate was $125 per hour to record. Donda did not have that much money. But Kanye kept asking around. Finally he found a recording studio that only charged $25 an hour. Donda agreed to pay to have the song recorded. She remembered, "The mic Kanye was to rap into was hanging from a wire clothes hanger, just sort of dangling there." But Kanye did not care. She described him as "in producer's heaven."

By Christmastime in 1991, Kanye had saved up $500. He wanted a keyboard, turntable, and mixer. So Donda gave Kanye $1,000 more for Christmas. He used the $1,500 to buy the equipment. Kanye could record his own music at home.

Kanye bought his first mixer, turntable, and keyboard in his teens.

Kanye attended Polaris High School in Oak Lawn, Illinois. He was an honor student in his first two years of high school. But by his junior year, his interest in art and music distracted him from other classes. He was winning art competitions and recording great music. But he was getting poor grades. Donda had to pay for a tutor to help Kanye pass some of his classes.

While he was in high school, Kanye met producer No I.D. He taught Kanye how to sample music and record over it. Kanye's music got better and better with No I.D.'s lessons.

When Kanye graduated from high school, he got a scholarship to the American Academy of Art in Chicago. He went to school there for a year before dropping out. Then he enrolled at Chicago State University where his mother taught. But soon he convinced his parents to let him drop out. He told Donda, "Mom, I can do this, and I don't need to go to college because I've had a professor in the house with me my whole life."

Kanye did have talent. The year before, Sony Records flew him to New York to audition. They paid for his plane ticket, a limousine to drive him around, and a hotel room. Then he met with the company executives. They asked Kanye what he did that was different from other hip-hop artists. Kanye had no answer for them. When they asked what he could offer the record company, Kanye told them that he would be bigger than their star, Jermaine Dupri. Unfortunately, one of the executives was Jermaine Dupri's father. Kanye left Sony without a record deal. He even had to get his own ride back to the airport.

Producer No I.D. taught Kanye about sampling and recording music.

Donda gave Kanye her blessing to drop out. She said, "It was drummed into my head that college is the ticket to a good life, but some career goals don't require college … It was more about having the guts to embrace who you are, rather than following the path society has carved out for you. And that's what Kanye did."

Kanye focused on making music. He made tracks of samples with his own beat recorded over them. He sold many beats to drug dealers who wanted to become rap stars. He could make $250 for each track he sold.

Since Kanye was not in school, Donda made him pay $200 rent every month. He was not making enough money selling his tracks, so he had to find a job. Kanye worked as a clerk at The Gap and then sold insurance over the phone. Kanye remembered, "I was way better than most of the people there. I could sit around and draw pictures, basically do other [things] while I was reading the teleprompter."

Kanye worked at his job during the day and made music at night. He had musician friends join him at the house. Donda grew tired of having people in her house late at night, and the music was too loud. She made Kanye find his own apartment.

A Chicago rapper named Gravity landed a record deal. Gravity bought one of Kanye's beats for $8,000 to include on the record. Then Ma$e, a rapper with Bad Boy Records, heard Kanye's beats. He started buying tracks from him too. Soon Kanye had enough money to move to New York. He wanted to be where there were more opportunities in hip-hop.

The rapper Ma$e bought many of Kanye's songs.

17

Big Name Acts

Kanye started working with bigger-name musicians. In 1998 Jermaine Dupri bought one of his beats for his album *Life in 1472*. The album reached number five on the *Billboard* 200 album charts.

Kanye was even busier in 1999. He produced a song for Foxy Brown's *Chyna Doll* album. It was the first hip-hop album by a female artist to reach number one on the *Billboard* 200 the week it came out. Kanye produced three songs on Harlem World's *The Movement*. Jermaine Dupri and the Trackmasters also produced songs on the album. Being on the same album as major record producers helped improve Kanye's status. Another important album for Kanye in 1999 was The Madd Rapper's *Tell 'Em Why U Madd*. He produced six of the songs on the album. His songs featured Ma$e, Jermaine Dupri, and Eminem. Then he followed up by producing a song on *The Notorious K.I.M.* by Lil Kim. Kanye was becoming a common name on some of the best hip-hop albums of the late 1990s.

Being well-known behind the scenes is not the same as being famous. Most people in New York had no idea who Kanye West was. One day someone pulled up next to him and asked about his car. It was Oprah Winfrey. Kanye introduced himself and told her he was a rapper. He explained that they were both from Chicago and said that one day he would be on her show. Later, Oprah recalled the conversation. She told Kanye, "People say that to me all the time. But you're the first person that ever made that true!"

Kanye produced songs along with well-known producers like Jermaine Dupri.

Roc-a-Fella Records heard Kanye's music and asked that he produce a track on Jay-Z's 2000 album, *The Dynasty: Roc la Familia*. Kanye worked with Jay-Z, Beanie Sigel, and Scarface on the song "This Can't Be Life." Jay-Z and Damon Dash were so impressed with Kanye's work that they signed him to produce a number of Roc-a-Fella songs the next year.

Kanye had a signature sound in the songs he produced. He would take hit music from the 1970s and speed them up. He heard the sound on the Wu-Tang Clan's music and used the idea on his own. Some people called his musical style "chipmunk soul" for the way the singer's voices sounded on his samples.

Roc-a-Fella signed Kanye to produce two songs on Beanie Sigel's 2001 album, *The Reason*. The album reached number five on the *Billboard* 200 charts. Then they asked him to produce five songs on Jay-Z's *The Blueprint*. Two of the songs, "Izzo (H.O.V.A.)" and "Girls, Girls, Girls," landed in the top twenty of the *Billboard* Hot 100 singles chart. The album reached number one on the album chart. *Rolling Stone* magazine named the album one of the best of all time. Working on the album together forged a strong friendship between Kanye and Jay-Z.

Jay-Z's career took off with the success of the album. Some people credited Kanye for saving Jay-Z's career. Kanye became one of the most sought-after record producers in the hip-hop industry after the success of *The Blueprint*. But Kanye wanted to do more than produce.

Kanye signed with Damon Dash at Roc-a-Fella Records.

Kanye wanted to rap, not just produce. As a producer, he did not have a contract with Roc-a-Fella. They just hired him when they needed him. So did many other record companies. Because he did not have a contract, Kanye could talk to any record company and try to get a recording contract.

Kanye tried first with Roc-a-Fella. They let him rap a few lines on songs they put out, but no more than that. When Roc-a-Fella artists performed at Madison Square Garden, Kanye asked to perform with them. Instead he was given two tickets to the show. From his seat, he was forced to watch people perform the music he made for them.

So Kanye started shopping around. He went back to Sony Records. He talked to executives at Def Jam and Arista Records. They told him that they would be happy to use him as a producer, but they just did not see him as a rapper. Capital Records came very close to signing him, but then changed their mind. Record companies wanted rappers with bad reputations. Former gangsters and drug dealers had the street-tough reputation that went along with hip-hop. Kanye grew up in a middle-class neighborhood. He lived in the suburbs. He was preppy. Nobody could be more opposite of a typical hip-hop star.

Even though they were friends, Jay-Z was not eager to see Kanye make records. In an interview, he said, "We all grew up street guys who had to do whatever we had to do to get by. Then there's Kanye, who to my knowledge has never hustled a day in his life. I didn't see how it could work."

Kanye produced songs for Roc-a-Fella artists like Young Gunz.

Crash!

Kanye kept pushing for a contract. He said, "I was mad because I was not being taken seriously as a rapper for a long time. Whether it was because I didn't have a larger-than-life persona, or I was perceived as the guy who made beats, I was disrespected as a rapper." Roc-a-Fella's Damon Dash remembered, "Kanye wore a pink shirt with the collar sticking up and Gucci loafers. It was obvious we were not from the same place or cut from the same cloth."

Kanye was badly injured in a car accident.

Kanye believed that he had what it took to be successful. He only needed a record company to take a chance on him. He said, "I had to hustle in my own way. I can't tell you how frustrating it was that they didn't get that. No joke—I'd leave meetings crying all the time."

Kanye produced over twenty songs in 2002. He traveled to Los Angeles to work with some West Coast artists. He often worked late into the night. While he drove home one October morning, he fell asleep. Kanye crashed head-on into another car. He nearly died.

The air bag did not go off, so his face hit the steering wheel. He watched in the rearview mirror as his face swelled to almost twice its normal size. He jaw was broken in three places. But Kanye and the other driver were both lucky to be alive. Later Kanye said, "When I had my accident, I found out at that moment nothing in life is promised except death. If you have the opportunity to play this game of life, you need to appreciate every moment."

Doctors had to wire Kanye's jaw shut in order for it to heal. The experience inspired Kanye to write the song "Through the Wire." It was based on Chaka Khan's hit song, "Through the Fire." Then he called Damon Dash. "He called me from his hospital bed with his jaw wired shut and asked for a drum machine," remembered Dash. "That impressed me."

Just weeks after the accident, Kanye went into the studio. He recordeded "Through the Wire." He still had his jaw wired shut. He was in so much pain that he was taking painkillers to get through the recording.

The accident helped Kanye become a better musician. He said, "I think I was just moving too fast ... I had too many things on my plate. And [the crash] allowed me to slow down and just focus on making really good music, which I think is my calling."

Roc-a-Fella finally agreed that Kanye was as good a performer as a producer.

Kanye made a mixtape of "Through the Wire" and some of the hit songs that he produced. Then he sent a copy to every record executive that would listen to it. Finally record companies were interested in Kanye as a rapper. Jay-Z and Damon Dash saw that other record companies were interested in him. Roc-A Fella offered him $150,000 to sign a recording contract with them. Kanye accepted the offer and started working on an album of his own.

Kanye started writing and recording songs for his album. At the same time, he was still producing records for other artists. Kanye was now one of rap's top producers. He had songs on fifteen albums in 2003 alone. He scored number-one hits on Ludacris's *Chicken-N-Beer* and Alicia Keys's *The Diary of Alicia Keys*.

Kanye worked on his own album as much as he could. Unfortunately, someone leaked the album months before it was supposed to come out. Instead of being mad, Kanye came up with a plan. He reworked his songs. He removed some songs that were supposed to be on the album.

Jamie Foxx sang with Kanye on a song from *The College Dropout*.

He replaced them with others that nobody had heard. He changed the songs that he kept on the album. He added new verses and a gospel choir. The people who got the leaked version of the album would buy something completely different when the actual album went on sale.

Kanye asked a number of rap artists to perform with him on the album. Common, who was also from Chicago, appeared on a song. Ludacris and Mos Def did too. Actor and singer Jamie Foxx sang on one of the songs that would be a single on the album. Foxx said, "That record restored my faith in hip-hop."

The album *The College Dropout* was finally released in February 2004. Many people thought that Kanye's music was a great answer to rap's gangster reputation. The songs were about religion, family, and personal struggle. He described it this way: "My persona is that I'm the regular person. Just think about whatever you've been through in the past week, and I have a song about that on my album."

The College Dropout sold over 400,000 copies in its first week. "Through the Wire" was on the *Billboard* Hot 100 chart for twenty-one weeks. The second single, "Slow Jamz," became Kanye's first number-one hit. *The College Dropout* sold over four million copies around the world.

Kanye's music was a hit with audiences. Critics loved the album too. Kanye tried to explain what made his music special. He said, "I was expressing what I was going through. All the better artists—I don't want to use the word 'great' because it'll come off as arrogant or whatever—all the better artists in history have expressed what they were going through." But with his confidence, Kanye also had complaints. He did not think that Roc-a-Fella spent enough on advertising. He was upset that more magazines did not put him on their covers. He did not think critics praised him strongly enough.

In November Kanye was at the American Music Awards (AMAs). He was nominated for Favorite Breakthrough Artist along with Maroon 5 and Gretchen Wilson. When Gretchen Wilson won the award, Kanye stormed off. He said, "I felt like I was definitely robbed ... I was the best new artist this year." He also swore he would never return to the AMAs.

In early 2004 he attended the Grammy Awards. *The College Dropout* received ten nominations. Kanye was asked to perform. He rapped about the people who hated him and tried to ruin his career. When he won the award for Best Rap Album, his speech was very arrogant. He said, "A lot of people were wondering what I was going to do if I didn't win anything ... I guess we'll never know."

Kanye kept performing and producing.

Kanye's friend Jay-Z retired briefly from music and became president of Def Jam Recordings. Def Jam then bought Roc-a-Fella Records. So Kanye was now recording for Def Jam, not Roc-a-Fella. The company was so pleased with Kanye's success that they gave him his own record label. Kanye called it "GOOD Music." It stood for "Get Out Our Dreams."

Kanye knew exactly who he wanted to work with. He signed his friend Common early on. Kanye also worked with some unknown musicians on *The College Dropout*. One was a singer and keyboard player named John Legend. Kanye signed John to a contract and helped him make his first album, *Get Lifted*. John went on to win three Grammy Awards for his debut.

Even with his own record label, Kanye kept working with artists on other labels. He worked with Janet Jackson, Twista, Jadakiss, Brandy, and over a dozen other artists. Kanye may have been known for being arrogant, but he knew how to make hit music.

Kanye was also influencing the way people dressed. He calls himself "The Louis Vuitton Don" after the luxury brand. In a music video, he wore a pink polo shirt and a Louis Vuitton backpack. When the videos came out, men started wearing pink polo shirts and carrying Louis Vuitton backpacks too.

The designer fashions were not typical for hip-hop stars. But it worked well for Kanye. His polished look and thoughtful lyrics were very different from rap's gangster image. So he was able to sell to people who liked the rhythm of hip-hop. And he reached new fans who liked his look and the ideas in his music.

New Sounds

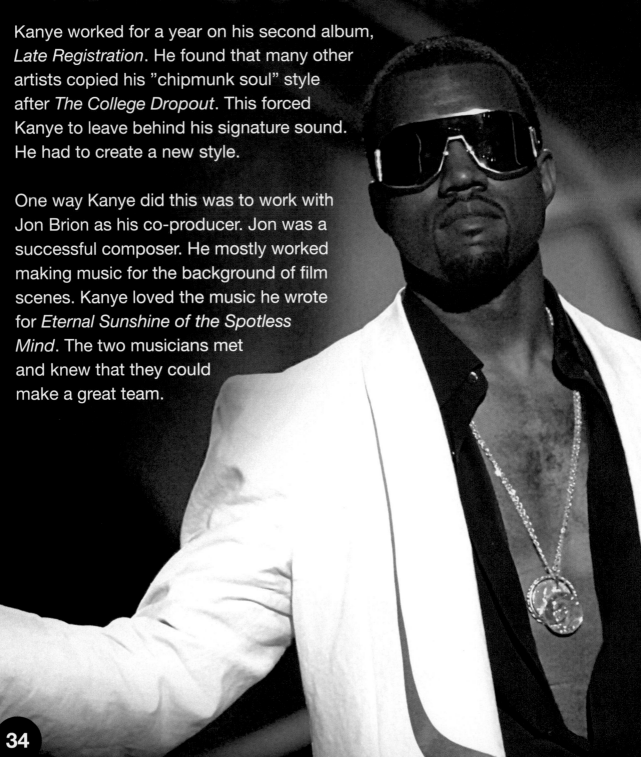

Kanye worked for a year on his second album, *Late Registration*. He found that many other artists copied his "chipmunk soul" style after *The College Dropout*. This forced Kanye to leave behind his signature sound. He had to create a new style.

One way Kanye did this was to work with Jon Brion as his co-producer. Jon was a successful composer. He mostly worked making music for the background of film scenes. Kanye loved the music he wrote for *Eternal Sunshine of the Spotless Mind*. The two musicians met and knew that they could make a great team.

One of the new approaches Kanye would take with *Late Registration* was to use a full orchestra. The sound was definitely not your average hip-hop sound. But Kanye was willing to take a chance to make his music stand out. He said, "I didn't want to play it boring and safe." But Kanye also wrote songs the way he had before. He rapped about issues like drug use and injustices. He explained, "I also didn't want to innovate too much. Second albums, man, they're even scarier than first ones."

Kanye released *Late Registration* in August 2005. It debuted at number one on the *Billboard* 200 album chart. He sold over two million copies of the album in the United States that year alone. Critics also loved the album. *Rolling Stone*, *Time*, and *Spin* magazines all named the album the best of 2005.

This album was also a success at the Grammys. It earned eight nominations. Kanye won for Best Rap Album, Best Rap Song, and Best Rap Solo Performance.

Kanye won three Grammy Awards for *Late Registration*.

Kanye toured with Irish rock band U2 in 2006. The band is known for being very active in social issues. They also wrote music that sounded fabulous in large concert arenas. Kanye changed his musical style again to include some of U2's style with his own. He also started experimenting with the electronic music that was popular in the 1980s.

With these new sounds, Kanye was ready to put out his third album. His record company announced that *Graduation* would be released in the summer of 2007. Another rapper, 50 Cent, was releasing an album the same month. In a bold move, 50 Cent said that if *Graduation* sold more copies than his album, he would quit recording. Kanye did not like the idea of a contest. He said, "I thought that was the stupidest thing. When my album drops and 50's album drops, you're gonna get a lot of good music at the same time."

Kanye eventually accepted the challenge and moved his release to the same day as 50 Cent's album. The contest would cause fans to buy albums just to take part in the competition. More sales meant more money. Kanye had nothing to lose even if 50 Cent won the challenge.

But Kanye had nothing to worry about. In its first week *Graduation* sold over 950,000 copies. This was over 266,000 more than 50 Cent's album sold in the same week.

In the same month he had his huge success, Kanye had another embarrassment. He was nominated for five different awards. He was also asked to perform at the MTV Video Music Awards, but not the show's opening number. That honor went to Britney Spears. Kanye lost all of the awards he was nominated for. After the show, he said that MTV was racist to let Britney Spears open the show instead of him. He also said that he would not come to the MTV awards again.

The rapper 50 Cent challenged Kanye to see who would sell more albums.

Just two months after the huge success of *Graduation*, Kanye suffered a huge loss. His mother, Donda, died. She was having plastic surgery in Los Angeles. She had visited a doctor before the surgery. He told her that she had a problem with her heart that could cause problems during the surgery. He told her to see another doctor about her heart condition. She did not. Instead she found another doctor who would perform the plastic surgery. As the first doctor predicted, her heart gave out after the surgery.

Kanye blamed himself for his mother's death. He felt that his fame was the problem. Donda had given up her teaching career to become his manager. This put her in the spotlight too. Kanye felt that she had the plastic surgery to look better when she was with him.

After her death, Kanye went on tour. He performed "Hey Mama" from *Late Registration* at every concert. He dedicated the song to her. It talked about how much she meant to him and how much she sacrificed to raise him. Kanye was also asked to perform at the 2008 Grammys. He again performed "Hey Mama."

Losing his mother shook up Kanye's life. He broke up with fiancée, Alexis Phifer. Then he went to Hawaii for three weeks. He recorded his next album there, *808s & Heartbreak*. He said the music was pop instead of hip-hop. It gave him a chance to say things that he found too hard to do with rap. The songs talked about how lonely he felt. The album also marked another musical style. Kanye used an autotune machine to give the voices and music a more digital sound.

Kanye broke up with Alexis Phifer.

Making More Music

Kanye took almost two years off after *808s & Heartbreak*. He moved to Oahu, Hawaii, and avoided making any music. He also avoided making public appearances. Then in November 2010 he released *My Beautiful Dark Twisted Fantasy*.

Kanye used three recording studios at a time to make the album. He would go to one studio and work on one song. When he ran out of ideas for that song, he would go to the next studio. There he would work on a different song. He went back and forth between the rooms, working on three songs at a time. He often stayed in the studio day and night. He took naps when he was tired. But he had people there ready to work twenty-four hours a day.

The album debuted at number one on the *Billboard* 200 album chart and stayed on the chart for thirty-two weeks. Some music critics said it was Kanye's best album. Many magazines called it the best album of 2010.

The next year, Kanye recorded *Watch the Throne* with Jay-Z. The friends had worked together on and off since Kanye produced *The Blueprint* for Jay-Z years ago. They first thought that they would make a five-song EP. But they kept writing more music until they had a full album. They earned a Grammy Award for the single "Otis."

After the release of the album, Jay-Z and Kanye went on tour. They performed fifty-seven shows in eight months. The two singers performed their many hit songs. The stage show included lasers, videos, and huge balls of fire. The tour sold over $48 million in tickets.

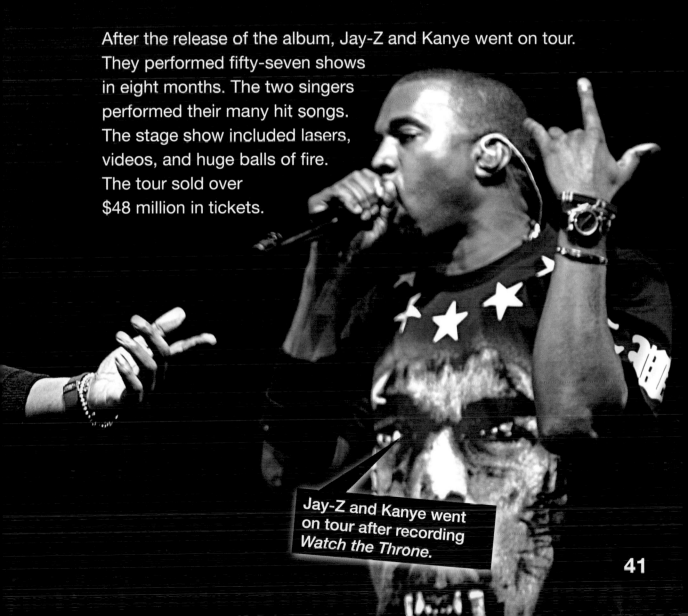

Jay-Z and Kanye went on tour after recording *Watch the Throne.*

Clearly, Kanye has had a huge musical career. But he has also built a huge career in design. He wrote a fashion column for *Complex* magazine. He also started his own design companies.

Starting in 2004, Kanye talked about designing clothes. He wore polo shirts with *The College Dropout* logo on it. Then he talked about deals that his company, Pastelle, would make with other designers. He wore clothes with the logo. He even appeared in a magazine spread with the singer Rihanna modeling the clothes. But the Pastelle line never made it to stores.

The failure of Pastelle did not end Kanye's fashion dreams. He worked with Nike to design a line of shoes, Air Yeezy. Then he worked with Louis Vuitton to design a line of athletic shoes. He had a two-year contract with them to design, but they did not make any of his designs after the first year.

Next Kanye applied for an internship with the European fashion designer Fendi. He worked there for four months. He had to use a different name and look so he would not be recognized. He worked with Fendi on men's clothing and learned how women's shoes were made.

In 2011 Kanye held a fashion show in Paris with a collection of his women's clothing. The reviews were not good. One fashion critic complained about one outfit in particular. She said, "The only thing more painful than witnessing the dress was watching the model pitch down the runway in shoes so ill-fitting that her spike heels were bending at angles." Kanye held another show in Paris in 2012, again with bad reviews. He was accused of using the style of other famous designers. The same critic said, "Ten points off for copying the smart guy sitting next to you."

Kanye designs women's fashions.

Kanye has offended a lot of people. He dressed as Jesus on the cover of *Rolling Stone* magazine. While raising money for victims of Hurricane Katrina, he said "George Bush doesn't care about black people." And in 2009 Taylor Swift won the award for Best Female Video. During her acceptance speech, Kanye took her microphone and said, "I'm sorry, but Beyoncé had one of the best videos of all time." Kanye apologized for his many instances of bad behavior. He gets invited back to award shows. President Bush and Taylor Swift have both accepted his apologies.

Kanye started dating Kim Kardashian.

Many women do not mind Kanye's attitude. He dated designer Alexis Phifer for six years. They became engaged in 2006 and broke up eighteen months later. After that, he dated models Brooke Crittenden, Amber Rose, and Melody Thornton. He is often photographed by paparazzi when he is out on dates.

Now Kanye is dating reality star Kim Kardashian. They started dating shortly after she filed for divorce from her husband, professional basketball star Kris Humphries. Kanye said, "I admit I fell in love with Kim ... 'round the same time she fell in love with him."

With his hit music career, Kanye has a lot to brag about. And he does not mind doing so. He says, "In America, they want you to accomplish these great feats ... But let someone ask you about what you're doing, and if you turn around and say, 'It's great,' then people are like, 'What's wrong with you?' You want me to be great, but you don't ever want me to say I'm great?"

Kanye interrupted Taylor Swift's awards speech.

Vocabulary

autotune	(adjective)	digitally corrected sound
Billboard	(noun)	magazine that covers the music industry, including record and album sales
contract	(noun)	an agreement between two people, between two companies, or between a person and a company
critic	(noun)	a person who judges
debut	(noun)	someone's first appearance
EP	(noun)	an extended play recording, usually longer than a single but shorter than an album
generation	(noun)	a group of people born about the same time
Grammy Award	(noun)	an award given to the best recording artists every year by The Recording Academy
hip-hop	(adjective or noun)	using strong beats and chanted words; music that uses strong beats and chanted words
internship	(noun)	a job that does not pay but provides experience
lyrics	(noun)	words to a song
mixtape	(noun)	a CD of songs made without a record company
nominate	(verb)	to suggest that someone might deserve an award
plastic surgery	(noun)	surgery that changes a person's appearance

pop	(adjective)	generally appealing; a watered-down version of rock and roll
producer	(noun)	a person who raises money to create a song, a stage show, and so on
profanity	(noun)	swearing or other inappropriate language
rap	(adjective, verb, or noun)	spoken with rhythm; to speak with rhythm; music in which words are spoken in rhythm
sample	(verb)	to take parts of songs and combine them with new music
segregation	(noun)	the separation of people by race, class, or other group
single	(noun)	one song, usually from an album
synesthesia	(noun)	a condition where a person gets more sensory information than normal
tabloid	(noun)	a celebrity gossip magazine
teleprompter	(noun)	a computer that provides the script for telephone workers

Photo Credits